If you were a

Contraction

Could n~~o~~t
Couldn't

Would n~~o~~t
Wouldn't

by Trisha Speed Shaskan
illustrated by Sara Gray

PICTURE WINDOW BOOKS
Minneapolis, Minnesota

contraction a word made by combining two words and leaving out a letter or letters

Editor: Christianne Jones
Designer: Hilary Wacholz
Page Production: Melissa Kes
Art Director: Nathan Gassman
The illustrations in this book were created with acrylics.

Picture Window Books
151 Good Counsel Drive
P.O. Box 669
Mankato, MN 56002-0669
877-845-8392
www.picturewindowbooks.com

Printed in the United States of America.

All books published by Picture Window Books
are manufactured with paper containing at least
10 percent post-consumer waste.

Library of Congress Cataloging-in-
Publication Data
Shaskan, Trisha Speed, 1973-
If you were a contraction / by Trisha Speed Shaskan ;
illustrated by Sara Gray.
p. cm. — (Word fun)
Includes bibliographical references and index.
ISBN 978-1-4048-4772-9 (library binding)
ISBN 978-1-4048-4775-0 (paperback)
1. English language—Contraction—Juvenile literature.
I. Gray, Sara., ill. II. Title.
PE1161.S56 2008
428.1—dc22
                        2008006353

Looking for contractions?
Watch for the BIG words throughout the book.

Special thanks to our advisers for their expertise:
Rosemary G. Palmer, Ph.D., Department of Literacy
College of Education, Boise State University

Terry Flaherty, Ph.D., Professor of English
Minnesota State University, Mankato

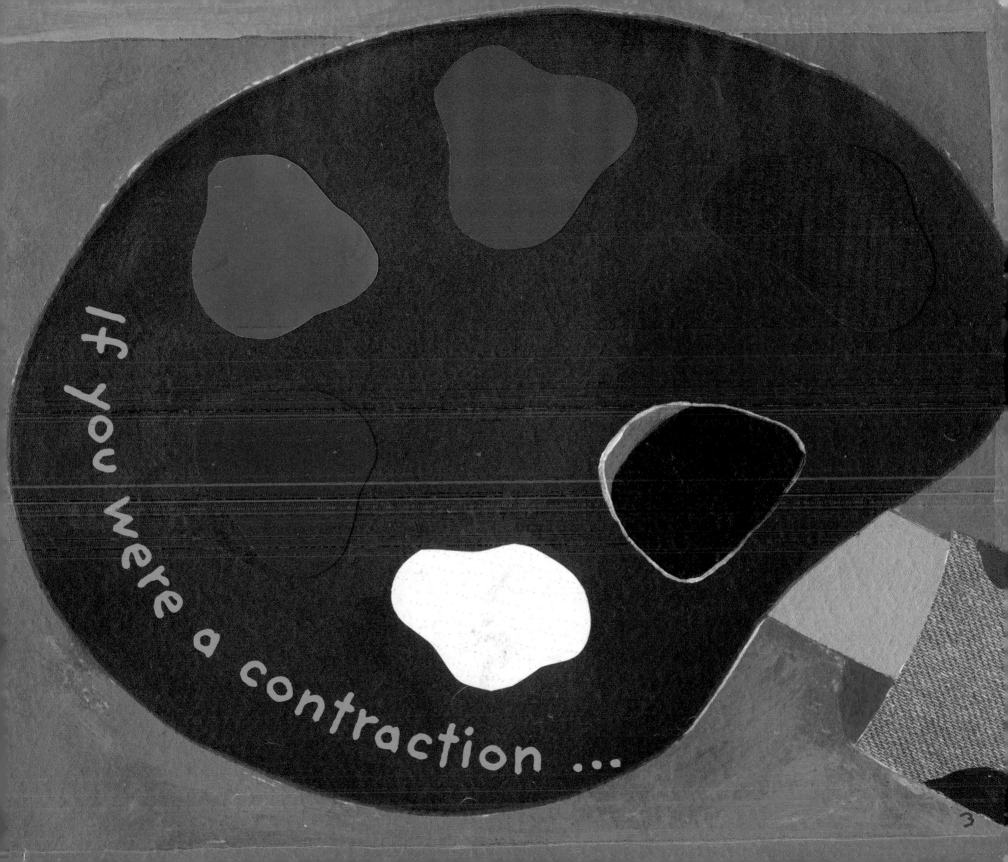

If you were a contraction ...

... your best friend would be the apostrophe!

You would change "could not" to **COULDN'T** and "would not" to **WOULDN'T.**

Could n~~o~~t
Couldn't

Would n~~o~~t
Wouldn't

If you were a contraction, you would be made by combining two words and leaving out a letter or letters. You would use an apostrophe to take the place of the missing letter or letters.

"**WHO'S** going to the store?" Mama asks.

"**I'M** going," says Papa.

"**I'M** going," says Sister.

If you were a contraction, you could add the word "not" to another word.

"Papa, **DON'T** hog the pancakes.
You SHOULDN'T overeat,"
Mama said.

"Do not" becomes **DON'T**.
"Should not" becomes **SHOULDN'T**.
"Would not" becomes **WOULDN'T**.

8

"DON'T worry. I WOULDN'T dream of it," Papa said.

If you were a contraction, you could add the word "is" to another word.

"**WHO'S** missing a hat?" Mama asked.

"Who is" becomes **WHO'S**.
"Where is" becomes **WHERE'S**.
"It is" becomes **IT'S**.

"I am," Sister said. "WHERE'S my hat now?"
"It's right here," Brother said.

If you were a contraction, you could add the word "are" to another word.

The family enjoys the beach. THEY'RE building a sand sculpture.

12

"WE'RE creating a piece of art!"
Sister exclaimed.
"And YOU'RE all dirty!" Papa said.

"They are" becomes THEY'RE.
"We are" becomes WE'RE.
"You are" becomes YOU'RE.

If you were a contraction, you could pair the pronoun "I" with another word.

"I am" becomes I'M.
"I will" becomes I'LL.
"I would" becomes I'D.

"I'M wearing my rubber boots so I can splash in the puddles!" Sister says.

"I'LL wear my raincoat," Brother says.

"I'D wear rubber boots and a coat," Papa says.

If you were a contraction, you could talk about the past. You could explain what did and did not happen.

The Pigs HADN'T cleaned the house for a long time.

"Had not" becomes HADN'T.
"Should have" becomes SHOULD'VE.
"Would have" becomes WOULD'VE.
"Could have" becomes COULD'VE.

"We **SHOULD'VE** remembered to take out the trash," Mama said.

"It **WOULD'VE** helped with the smell," Papa said.

"It **COULD'VE** helped with the bugs, too," Brother said.

"**I'M** having cookies," Brother says.
"**I'M** having popcorn," Sister says.
"**LET'S** have pasta," Mama says.
Everyone says, "**THAT'S** a great idea!"

"Let us" becomes **LET'S.**
"That is" becomes **THAT'S.**

If you were a contraction, you could take place in the future.

Papa says HE'LL learn to play the trombone.
Sister says SHE'LL learn to play the trumpet.

"He will" becomes HE'LL.
"She will" becomes SHE'LL.
"They will" becomes THEY'LL.

Mama says **SHE'LL** learn to be a singer.
Brother says **HE'LL** learn to play the piano.
THEY'LL be one fun family band!

21

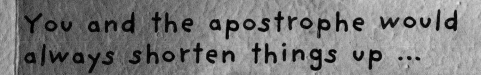

You and the apostrophe would always shorten things up ...

... if you were a contraction.

FUN WITH CONTRACTIONS

To form a contraction, all you have to do is combine two words and leave out a letter or letters. Grab a piece of paper and change the words below into contractions. After you've created contractions, use each one in a sentence. You could write sentences about your family or about your friends.

1. I am =

2. you will =

3. it is =

4. she is =

5. we are =

6. is not =

7. he would =

8. they have =

Glossary

apostrophe—the mark used to take the place of one or more letters in a contraction

contraction—a word made by combining two words and leaving out a letter or letters

future—about to happen

past—already happened

present—happening now

pronoun—a word that takes the place of a noun

To Learn More

More Books to Read

Carr, Jan. *Greedy Apostrophe: A Cautionary Tale.* New York: Holiday House, 2007.

Cooper, Barbara. *Alan Apostrophe.* Milwaukee: Gareth Stevens, 2005.

Truss, Lynne. *The Girl's Like Spaghetti: Why, You Can't Manage without Apostrophes!* New York: G.P. Putnam's Sons, 2007.

On the Web

FactHound offers a safe, fun way to find Web sites related to topics in this book. All of the sites on FactHound have been researched by our staff.

1. Visit www.facthound.com
2. Type in this special code: 1404847723
3. Click on the FETCH IT button.

Your trusty FactHound will fetch the best sites for you!

Index

apostrophe, 4, 6, 22
contraction
  adding "are," 12–13
  adding "I," 14–15
  adding "is," 10–11
  adding "not," 8–9
  definition, 6
future tense, 20–21
past tense, 16–17
present tense, 18–19

Look for all of the books in the Word Fun series:

If You Were a Compound Word
If You Were a Conjunction
If You Were a Contraction
If You Were a Homonym or a Homophone
If You Were a Noun
If You Were a Palindrome
If You Were a Prefix
If You Were a Preposition
If You Were a Pronoun
If You Were a Suffix
If You Were a Synonym
If You Were a Verb
If You Were Alliteration
If You Were an Adjective
If You Were an Adverb
If You Were an Antonym
If You Were an Interjection
If You Were Onomatopoeia